CARL RÜTTI

THREE CAROLS

FOR SATB CHORUS & ORGAN

NOVELLO

Published by
Novello Publishing Limited
14-15 Berners Street,
London W1T 3LJ, UK.

Exclusive Distributors:
Music Sales Limited
Distribution Centre, Newmarket Road,
Bury St Edmunds, Suffolk IP33 3YB, UK.

Music Sales Corporation
257 Park Avenue South,
New York, NY 10010, USA.

Music Sales Pty Limited
20 Resolution Drive, Caringbah,
NSW 2229, Australia.

Order No. NOV016335
ISBN 978-1-84938-782-8

Music engraved by Chris Hinkins.
Illustration by Ruth Keating.

Printed in the EU.

A separate brass quintet accompaniment is available on sale from the publisher.
(2 trumpets in B flat, horn in F, trombone, tuba)
Order number: NOV016335-02

www.chesternovello.com

CONTENTS

Please note: *I wonder as I wander* in this edition differs from
the version published in Christmas at King's College, 2009 (NOV040073)

1. p.2, bar 20: 2nd note organ pedal, low A is now a quaver
   (was previously a crotchet)

2. p.3, bar 30: *t'was* in the voices is now a quaver,
   (was previously a crotchet) [organ part unaltered]

3. p.4, bar 40: 2nd note organ pedal, low A is now a quaver,
   (was previously a crotchet). The left hand chord 2nd beat is also a quaver.
   [The effect is the same in the manuals; the pedal note is shorter on the 2nd beat]

4. p.6, bar 60: 2nd note organ pedal, low A is now a quaver
   (was previously a crotchet)

Three Carols

Carl Rütti (b.1949)
Organ reduction by
Anne Duarte & Carl Rütti

John Jacob Niles

1. I wonder as I wander

sky,_____ how Je - sus the Sa - viour did come_____ for to die for

sky,_____ how Je - sus the Sa - viour did come_____ for to die for

sky,_____ how Je - sus the_ Sa - viour did_ come for to_ die for

sky,_____ how Je - sus the_ Sa - viour did_ come for to_ die for

poor on - 'ry peo - ple like you and like I._____ I won - der as I

poor on - 'ry peo - ple like you and like I._____ I won - der as I

poor on - 'ry peo - ple like you and like I._____ I won - der as I

poor on - 'ry peo - ple like you and like I._____ I won - der as I

wise men and far-mers and shep-herds and all. But high from the

wise men and far-mers and shep-herds and all. But high from the

wise men and_ far-mers and_ shep-herds and_ all. But high from the

wise men and_ far-mers and_ shep-herds and_ all. But high from the

hea-vens a star's light did fall,_____ and pro-mise of_ a-ges it

hea-vens a star's light did fall,_____ and pro-mise of_ a-ges it

hea-vens a star's light did fall,_____ and pro-mise of_ a-ges it

hea-vens a star's light did fall,_____ and pro-mise of_ a-ges

sky, or a bird_____ on the wing, or all of God's an-gels in

sky,_____ a bird_____ on the wing, or all of God's an-gels in

sky, or a_ bird on the_ wing, or all of God's an-gels in

sky, or a_ bird on the_ wing, or all of God's an-gels in

hea-ven for to sing,_____ he sure-ly could have it, 'cause he was the King.

hea-ven for to sing,_____ he sure-ly could have it, 'cause he was the King.

hea-ven for to sing,_____ he sure-ly could have it, 'cause he was the King.

hea-ven for to sing,_____ he sure-ly could have it, he was the King.

2. O little town of Bethlehem

Phillips Brooks

10

O morn-ing stars, to - ge - ther pro - claim the__ ho-ly Birth,

O morn-ing stars, to - ge - ther pro - claim the ho - ly Birth,

O morn-ing stars, to - ge - ther pro - claim the ho - ly Birth,

O morn-ing stars, to - ge - ther pro - claim the ho - ly Birth,

And prai-ses sing to God the King, and peace to

And prai-ses sing to God the King, and peace to

And prai-ses sing to God the King, and peace to

And prai - ses__ sing to God the King, and peace to

men on earth; For Christ is born of Ma -

men on earth; For Christ is born of Ma -

men on earth; For Christ is born of Ma -

men on earth; For Christ is born of Ma -

- ry; and, ga - thered____ all a - bove,_____ For Christ is born of

- ry; and, ga-thered all a - bove,_____ For Christ is born of

- ry; and, ga-thered all___ a - bove,_____ For Christ is born of

- ry; and, ga - thered all a - bove,_____ For Christ is born of

119

Cast out our sin, and en- ter in, be born in us to-

Cast out our sin, and en- ter in, be born in__ us to-

Cast out our sin, and en- ter in, be born in us__ to-

Cast out our sin, and en- ter in, be__ born in us to-

125

-day. We hear__ the

-day. We hear__ the

-day. We__ hear the Christ-

-day. We__ hear the Christ-

16

great glad_____ tid - ings tell;_____ O come to

great glad tid - ings tell;_____ O come to

great glad tid - ings tell;_____ O

great glad tid - ings tell;_____ come___

us, a - bide with us, our Lord Em - ma - nu - el.

us, a - bide with us,___ our Lord Em - ma - nu - el.

come to us,_____ a - bide with us,_____ Em - ma - nu - el.

___ to us, a - bide,_ our Lord Em - ma - nu - el.

18

3. My dancing day

Traditional English

21

Then was I born of a vir - gin pure; of her I_____

Then was I born of a vir - gin pure; of her,_____

Then was I born of a vir - gin pure; of her I_____

Then was I born of a vir - gin pure; of her I_____

took flesh - ly sub - stance. Thus was I knit to

___ of her,_____ Thus was I knit to

took flesh - ly sub - stance. Thus was I knit to

took of flesh - ly sub - stance. Thus was I knit to

man's na - ture, to call my true love to___ the dance.

man's na - ture, to call my true love to the dance.

man's na - ture, to call my true love to the dance.

man's na - ture, to call my true love to the dance.

Sing, sing, sing, sing, sing, sing,

Sing, sing, sing, sing, sing, sing,

Sing, sing, sing, sing, sing, sing,

O my love, O my

Man.

my true love.

my true love.

my true love.

my true love.

mf

Man.

In a man-ger laid and wrapped I was, so____

In a man-ger laid and wrapped I was, so

In a man-ger laid and wrapped I was, so____

In a man-ger laid and wrapped I was, so____

Ped.

31